BUGS!

By Patricia and Fredrick McKissack

Illustrated by Mike Cressy

Children's Press®
A Division of Grolier Publishing
New York • London • Hong Kong • Sydney
Danbury, Connecticut

To MaJon Carwell,
our nephew and happy reader.
—P. and F.M.

To my brothers: Claude (Nick), Kevin, and Scotty,
who occasionally bugged me when we were kids.
—M.C.

Reading Consultants
Linda Cornwell
Coordinator of School Quality and Professional Improvement
(Indiana State Teachers Association)

Katharine A. Kane
Education Consultant
(Retired, San Diego County Office of Education
and San Diego State University)

Visit Children's Press® on the Internet at:
http://publishing.grolier.com

Library of Congress Cataloging-in-Publication Data
McKissack, Pat.
   Bugs! / by Patricia and Fredrick McKissack; illustrated by Mike Cressy — Rev. ed.
     p . cm. — (Rookie reader)
   Summary: Simple text and illustrations of a variety of insects introduce the
numbers one through five.
    ISBN 0-516-21658-9 (lib.bdg.)   0-516-27046-X (pbk.)
    [1. Insects Fiction. 2. Counting.] I. McKissack, Fredrick. II. Cressy, Mike, ill.
III. Title. IV. Series.
PZ7.M478693Bu 2000
[E] — dc 21   99-15875
                                         CIP

GROLIER
PUBLISHING   2 3 4 5 6 7 8 9 10 R 09 08 07 06 05 04 03 02 01 00

Bugs.

3

Up here.

One fat red bug.

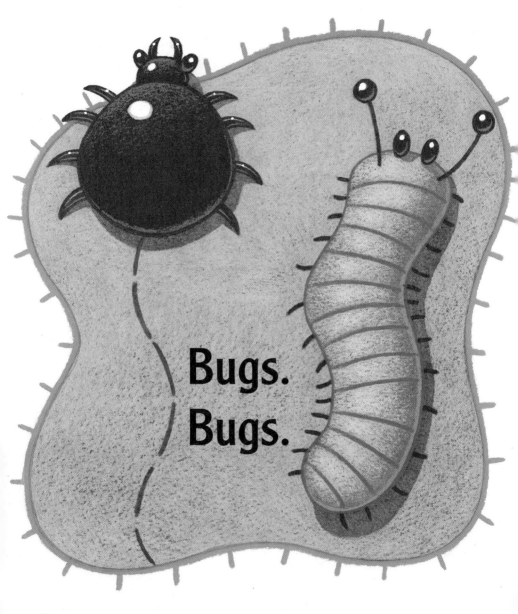

Bugs.
Bugs.

Where?

Under here.

Two long, skinny, yellow bugs.

Bugs.

Bugs.

Bugs.

Where?

Over there.

14

Three fat, green bugs with two big eyes.

Bugs. Bugs. Bugs. Bugs.

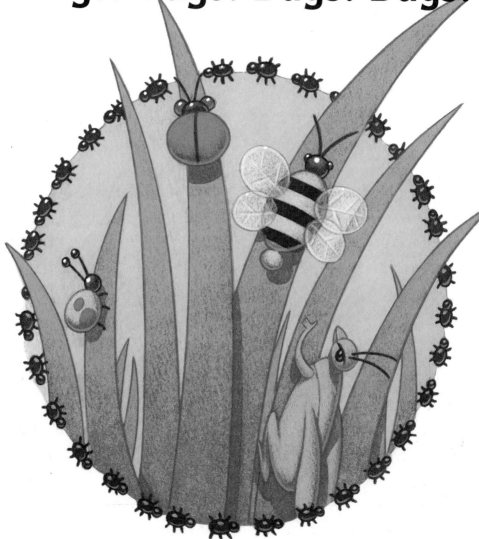

Where?

In here.

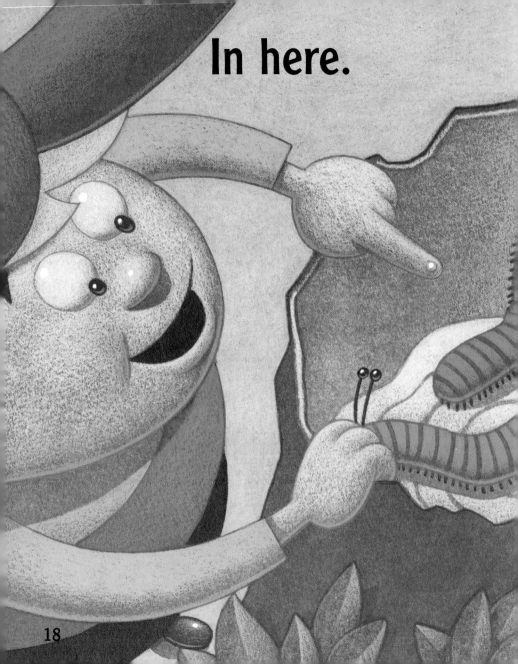

Four bugs with four hundred feet.

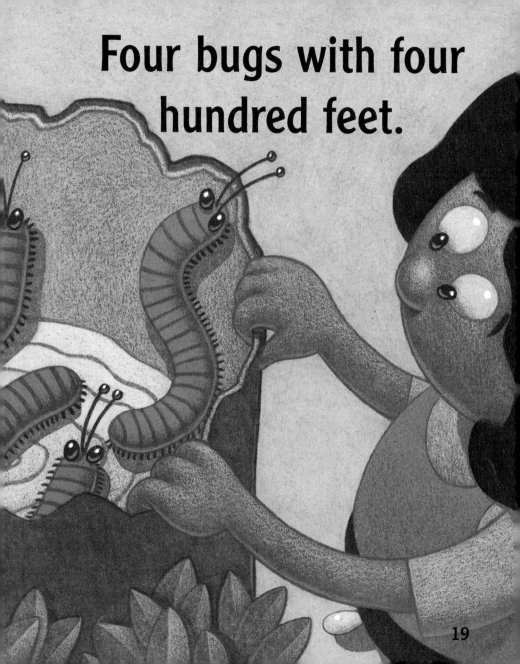

Bugs. Bugs. Bugs. Bugs. Bugs.

Where?

Out there.

Five little bugs that fly here and there.

Bugs. Bugs.

Lots of bugs.

Where?

Where?

Everywhere!

Word List (33 words)

and	green	red
big	here	skinny
bug	hundred	that
bugs	in	there
everywhere	little	three
eyes	long	two
fat	lots	under
feet	of	up
five	one	where
fly	out	with
four	over	yellow

About the Authors

Patricia and Fredrick McKissack are freelance writers and editors, living in St. Louis County, Missouri. Their awards as authors include the Coretta Scott King Award, the Jane Addams Peace Award, the Newbery Honor, and the 1998 Regina Medal from the Catholic Library Association. They have written numerous titles, including the *Messy Bessey* books, in the Rookie Reader series.

About the Illustrator

Mike Cressy works in the shadow of Seattle, occasionally peeking out to warm himself in the sun.